The Four Pearls and The Four Squirrels:

A Modern Fable About Happiness and Distraction

To Jenni —
With love,
Lissa Coffey

The FOUR PEARLS AND THE FOUR SQUIRRELS

A MODERN FABLE ABOUT HAPPINESS AND DISTRACTION

LISSA COFFEY

Bamboo Entertainment, Inc

For the
SEEKERS
And for the
GEMS -
One and the same.

Table of Contents

Foreword

The concept of a having a mentor goes back to ancient times. The word "mentor" actually comes from the character Mentor in Homer's Odyssey. In the book, the goddess Athena takes on the appearance of Mentor to guide a young Telemachus through some difficulty.

Mentorships can be found in many traditions, including the Gurus in Hinduism and Buddhism, and the Elders in Judaism and Christianity. Today mentors have become popular to help newcomers navigate through the business world. Big Brothers Big Sisters of America is a non-profit organization that provides one-on-one mentoring to children in need. In any case, the relationship is one in which a more experienced or knowledgeable person helps to guide a less experienced person. It is a kind of partnership that provides support and communication. And magnificent growth and insights can occur for both parties involved.

In my own life, I have had the gift of many able and inspired mentors. One who stands out was Edgar Mitchell, who was one of the Apollo 14 astronauts who walked on the moon, and a hero who braved great adventures in his career and his life. Over the several decades that I knew him, he modeled kindness, intelligence, and a great passion for the wellbeing of humanity. In particular, he had a rare gift of open-minded curiosity—combined with a commitment to rigor and discernment. Much like Mentor, who helped Telemachus in his coming of age journey, Edgar was a source of great inspiration in my own quest for truth and authenticity.

In The Four Pearls and The Four Squirrels the character of Merlinda acts as a kind of mentor to the four squirrels. She is kind and wise and gracefully presents a situation where the four squirrels can access both their inner strength, and the higher knowledge they each need to achieve their goals. Edgar Mitchell was this kind of mentor to me as I made my way into a career at the frontiers of science.

For those of us fortunate enough to have had mentors, we know what a difference such guidance can make in our lives. With this book, author Lissa Coffey has also taken on the role of mentor in bringing this sweet, clear, profound wisdom to her readers.

Ask yourself the same question that Merlinda asked the squirrels: "Do you want to be happy?" I encourage you to read The Four Pearls and the Four Squirrels, and to take the pearls of wisdom to heart. Share with your family, friends, and community. Carry these principles with you and see how they help you to experience greater clarity, peace of mind, and, yes, happiness. After all, when it comes down to it, isn't that we all really want?

 Marilyn Schlitz, Ph.D.

Author, researcher and speaker

Professor and Chair of the PhD programs in transpersonal psychology at Sofia University

President Emeritus and Senior Fellow, The Institute of Noetic Science

Introduction

A fable is a short story featuring animals that are given human qualities, such as the ability to speak. A fable could also include imaginary creatures, inanimate objects or things found in nature as well, any of which may have the qualities or abilities of a person. A fable is meant to illustrate a lesson, or a "moral" as a part of the story.

Fables are found in books from all over the world. Many of us remember hearing Aesop's fables read to us when we were in school. The tradition of storytelling is what helped fables last over the years, and spread over the continents. Aesop lived in Greece sometime around 550 BC, and his fables are still applicable to situations in our lives today. A person who writes fables is called a fabulist, and besides Aesop, some famous fabulists include: Leonardo da Vinci, Hans Christian Anderson, James Thurber, George Orwell, Dr. Seuss, David Sedaris, and Guillermo del Toro.

One of my very favorite books growing up was Jonathan Livingston Seagull by Richard Bach. It had a profound effect on me. I read it and re-read it countless times. The book, and the character of Jonathan, inspired me and stayed with me all these years.

The four pearls of wisdom are concepts that have helped me many times, in many different circumstances. I wanted to write a book that explained these concepts, and I wanted to have a way for the concepts to be remembered. Thinking of Jonathan, I decided to put the concepts in the form of a fable. And this is my first one.

In this fable, The Four Pearls and The Four Squirrels, we first meet Merlinda, a wizardess. Merlinda is the great-great-granddaughter of King Arthur's Merlin. She has remodeled the old family home in the forest using DIY tips she learned from HGTV, and just a little bit of magic.

The squirrels in the story are certainly family, but they may or may not be related to each other. As we know, this global world is becoming smaller and smaller. And as that happens, our family expands to include lots of friends who are like family to us. We're all connected, after all. We're all brothers and sisters. The squirrels are also not of any certain age. They could be children, or young adults, empty-nesters or retirees. It's up to the reader to imagine.

the Treasure Hunt Begins

Not so long ago, in a forest not so far away, lived a wise Wizardess named Merlinda. Merlinda loved living in the forest, with nature all around her. The fresh air allowed her to breathe freely. The quiet mist helped to settle her mind. The abundant gifts from the trees gave her shelter and nourishment. The forest animals provided friendly company.

As Merlinda was so kind and caring, the animals often came to her for advice. She was happy to give guidance, and loved being of service to her companions.

Among her favorite friends were four squirrels, brothers and sisters, who frolicked and played in Merlinda's backyard. This was great entertainment for Merlinda, who giggled at their antics.

One day, when Merlinda was busy in the kitchen, she was startled by a great commotion just outside her door. She swung the door open to see just what was going on. To her surprise, it was the four squirrels, quarreling and getting rather bossy with one another.

"Please, little ones!" Merlinda said with the utmost of patience. "Whatever has you so worked up this way?"

The four squirrels were frazzled and frustrated. The all spoke at once, loudly, and quickly:

"She started it!"

"He took my acorn!"

"They are being mean to me!"

"She bit my ear!"

"They ran away from me!"

"There's no more left!"

"He's doing it again!"

Merlinda couldn't make out a word they were saying, but she understood exactly what was going on. "Now, now, my dears. I have heard enough. Let's get to the bottom of this. Just answer a simple question for me, please."

The squirrels let out a few huffs of anger and exchanged some unfriendly faces with each other. But they did keep quiet as they braced themselves, each one secretly planning how he or she would present their case.

Merlinda's soothing voice abruptly changed the mood. "Do you want to be happy?" she asked with a sweet smile.

The squirrels looked confused. They didn't know how to respond.

Do you want to be happy?
Then you are ready to find the
four pearls.

"It's a simple question, darling squirrels. Most everyone wants to be happy. I'm just asking you if you want to be happy. Do you? You can think about it if you want."

"Well, yes, I want to be happy, of course," the first squirrel piped up. He was the big brother squirrel and he usually went first. "I just don't see what this has to do with anything!"

"Ah, it has to do with everything, my friend," Merlinda replied with her usual graciousness.

"I want to be happy, too!" chimed in the other squirrels. "Me, too!" "And me!"

"Well then, I think you are ready to find the four pearls," Merlinda answered back with confidence.

"Pearls? What pearls? Pearls in the forest? What's a pearl?" The squirrels were once again confused – but this time they were curious as well.

"I have hidden four precious pearls in the forest.

A pearl is the only gemstone that grows in beauty from the inside out. It is much like all of us.

As we learn and grow our kindness and wisdom shines through us." Merlinda looked at the little squirrels, who were now paying close attention to every word she was saying. "Find these four pearls and bring them back to me. When you do so you will be greatly rewarded."

The squirrels started squirming, as squirrels usually do, they could hardly sit still they were so excited. "Ok, ok, we're going on a hunt! Where do we start? How much time do we have?"

"There are no rules to this game. Just look for the pearls, and see what happens." Merlinda ushered them along and the four squirrels eagerly scampered through the trees deep into the forest.

the First Pearl

The little squirrels moved quickly, covering a lot of ground, searching for pearls amongst the fallen leaves and tufts of grass. It didn't take long before they got distracted by the butterflies fluttering by, and the birds singing to the sky.

"I'm hungry," said the younger of the sisters.

"I'm tired," said the little brother.

"This is boring," said the big sister.

"Why can't I fly like the butterfly? Then I could see from up high, and maybe I could just spot a pearl and go straight to it! I wish I had wings!"

"Ugh, I wish I had the voice of a bird. Then I could call in all the other animals to help me. They'd follow me around and find the pearl for me!" the little sister said.

The squirrels looked up towards the bird, who seemed to be laughing at them. "Ha, ha!" squawked the bird. "Such silly creatures! You aren't bolted to the ground! I've seen you climb the highest of trees to get even the smallest nut. You've never needed anyone's help. Do you forget who you are?"

Do you forget who you are?

"Wait! Bird! Are you saying a pearl is in the tree? Did you see one?" The squirrels scrambled up the tree to get closer to the bird, but the bird flew off, as a bird might do with four squirrels barreling after him.

From the highest branches, the squirrels could look down and see much of the forest.

"Wow," the little sister exclaimed. "I might not have wings like the butterfly, but I can surely see far from up here. I am so glad I have my sharp claws to climb the tree!"

"And I may not be able to sing, but I'm so glad I have my fluffy tail to help me balance. I see plenty of nuts out on these branches. Looks like lunchtime to me!" said the little brother.

The four squirrels munched on nuts until their bellies were full, then headed back down the tree.

The big brother squirrel paused for a moment before resuming the search.

"You know," he said as he addressed his siblings, "when I was young I couldn't climb trees like that. My claws were too soft. I had to practice, and keep trying before climbing became easy for me. It was a lot of work, but it was worth it. We've got skills, squirrels! I know we haven't found any of Merlinda's pearls yet, but we can do it. We just have to look at what we have, and not at what we don't have."

And with that statement, a perfect, beautiful little pearl fell from the tree and landed in his little squirrel hand.

"Look! Look!" the squirrels all squealed with delight. "It's a pearl! A real pearl! It must have come loose when we picked the nuts!"

"Well, what do you know?" the big brother grinned. "Let's go get the rest of them!" And they headed off on their journey once again.

THE First Pearl

Look at
WHAT
YOU HAVE,
Not at
WHAT YOU
DON'T HAVE.

FourPearlsBook.com

the Second Pearl

As the squirrels went about looking for the remaining pearls, they were once again easily distracted. This time it was by a chipmunk, gathering up a large pile of acorns into an old tree trunk. The squirrels darted over to find out what was going on. The chipmunk paid no attention to the squirrels and kept at his task. When he heard the squirrels whispering to each other, the chipmunk spoke up. "These are my acorns so don't get any ideas!" he bellowed, not missing a step in hiding his stash.

"But why?" said the little brother. "There are acorns all over this forest. Why do you need a pile in the trunk? It's not even close to winter."

"Oh, youngster, this is what I do. I like to have a stock of goods that I can go to when I need them. So be on your way, don't bother me anymore." The chipmunk seemed annoyed, so the squirrels left him alone with his acorns.

"Maybe we should do that," said the big sister. "I mean, wouldn't Merlinda be happy if we brought home a bunch of nuts and seeds instead of a pearl? You can't eat a pearl after all!"

"That's right!" said the little brother. "I would love to have a nice big pile of nuts and seeds that I could have around to eat anytime. That chipmunk is smart! We should do that instead!"

Just then their friend the bird flew by with leaves and twigs in his beak. The squirrels ran up the tree to say hello. "Whatcha doing, Bird? You can't sing with all this stuff in your mouth!" the little sister pointed out, as if he didn't know.

"You're certainly right there, little squirrel." The bird answered with much patience. "But I have a nest to make. I need somewhere to sleep at night, somewhere that my family can sleep, too."

"Ooooh! Maybe we should do that!" the big brother said to his siblings. "We need a nest, too. What if we want to take a nap out here?"

The little brother agreed quite readily. "Yes, that's a good point. In fact, I'm getting sleepy right now! Let's make a nest like the bird."

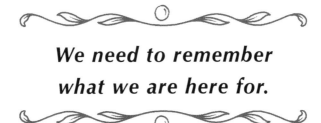

We need to remember what we are here for.

"No, no, no," the little sister said. "We need to remember what we are here for. If we start stacking acorns or building nests we will never find the pearls. We can't get distracted by all these other activities. We four squirrels are here to look for the four pearls. That is our job. We have to look at what we are doing, not at what anyone else is doing."

And with that bold statement, a beautiful round pearl dropped right into the little sister's hands. The squirrels could hardly believe their eyes. "It's so pretty! How can this be? It must have fallen from another bird's beak!" they speculated. With renewed excitement, they headed off to find the other two pearls.

THE Second Pearl

Look at
WHAT YOU
ARE DOING,
Not at
WHAT ANYONE
ELSE IS DOING.

FourPearlsBook.com

the Third Pearl

After a few hours, and a few more miles of searching high and low for the remaining two pearls, the four squirrels were starting to lose hope. "Where do we go now?" whined the little brother, "we've covered as far as we've ever been into the forest."

"That's true," the big sister said to the little guy. "But that doesn't mean we can't go further."

"I don't know about that," said the big brother. "We wouldn't want to get lost."

"We can make a map! Or we can leave a trail to follow back. There's no reason to be scared," big sister sounded very optimistic.

"But we don't know how to make a map. And I have never left a trail before," little brother said, worried that they might not get back home should they venture out too far.

"And besides that, there's a stream. How can we cross the stream?" little sister chimed in. "Squirrels don't swim."

"Have you ever tried?" big sister countered. "Look, you can come up with all kinds of excuses why we can't go further. But there's always a way. We can find a branch to crawl on, we can jump from rock to rock, we can help each other get across the stream."

"But what if we can't do it?" big brother interrupted. "What if...?"

"What if we can do it?" big sister exclaimed. "How much do we want these pearls? Isn't it worth it to take the risk? Isn't it worth it to stretch our abilities a bit?

Yes, there are obstacles in front of us. But maybe these obstacles are really opportunities.

We need to look at the opportunities, not at the obstacles."

Just as those words came out of her mouth, a precious, luminous pearl dropped into big sister's hand.

"What? Again? This can't be a co-incidence!" The squirrels pranced around in celebration. "We have three pearls! We have three pearls! One more to go!"

Emboldened with courage, the four squirrels made their way into the part of the forest that they'd never visited before.

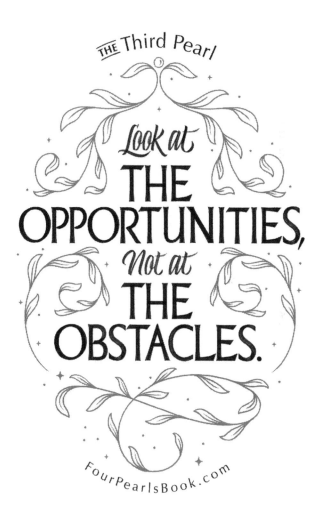

THE Third Pearl

Look at
THE
OPPORTUNITIES,
Not at
THE
OBSTACLES.

FourPearlsBook.com

the Fourth Pearl

The squirrels were a bit surprised to find that this part of the forest, though unknown to them, was much like the other part of the forest that was familiar to them. They didn't have trouble navigating around and they had a lot of fun exploring. Again, they went through the process of turning over leaves, crawling through brush, and looking high and low through the trees for the very last pearl. They were each quite involved in their pursuit, when little sister let out a "Squeeeeeeeeeal!" The other squirrels rushed to her side.

"Did you find it? Where is it?" big sister asked, catching her breath.

"I didn't find the pearl. I found something better!" little sister proclaimed proudly.

"What? What could be better than a pearl?" little brother puzzled.

"It's a DIAMOND!" little sister announced as she waved her hand in front of her treasure like a model on a TV game show. Her siblings stopped and stared, not sure what to make of this thing.

"It's a diamond. Like the rock that Merlinda wears on her finger. It's the same thing, see?

It's shiny!" Little sister was doing her best to convince them.

Just because it's shiny doesn't mean it's a diamond.

"Just because it's shiny doesn't mean it's a diamond," big sister stated very matter-of-factly. "You can't say something is real just because of how it looks."

Big brother took a good hard look at the clear rock in question. "I think it is a diamond! Diamonds are very valuable. Much more valuable than a pearl. And I think Merlinda would be very pleased if we brought it home to her," he said.

"Merlinda never said anything about a diamond. What would a diamond be doing in the forest anyway? She might not want it. But I want it!" little sister said trying hard to contain her excitement.

"If we're taking it then we can't look for the other pearl, we will have too much to carry. Let me see if I can pick up this diamond."

Little brother stepped up and reached out his little squirrel arms to lift the shiny rock. It was heavy for him, and as he struggled with it the shiny stone slipped from his grip and tumbled over onto a rock and broke.

"See!" big sister was always happy to point out when she was right. "A real diamond wouldn't break like that. It's just glass, a piece of broken glass, worth nothing."

"But it's so pretty!" little sister wailed.

"I could get that little piece for you," little brother said, wanting to make his sister happy. He bent down to pick up a chunk that had broken off. "Owwww!" he pulled his hand away quickly.

"Are you okay?" Big sister took his little hand in hers and saw that he had a cut.

Little sister looked so sad. "Oh, Brother I'm so sorry! You wanted to get the piece of glass for me; if I didn't want it you wouldn't have been hurt."

"He's fine," big brother said as he comforted his sister squirrel. "It's just a little cut. It will heal. Nothing lasts forever."

"That's not exactly true," little brother said shaking his head. "My cut will heal for sure. And that is definitely not a real diamond, but even diamonds don't last forever. This stone or glass or whatever it is, even if it was a diamond – it is just a "thing" and it is keeping us from finding the pearl. But there is something that is true and real and lasts forever."

The other squirrels looked at this littlest squirrel and saw strength and wisdom in his eyes.

"Okay, you tell us. Please tell us what it is that lasts forever," they encouraged him.

Love is always with us.

"It's love. Love is always with us. I know you all love me, that's why I wasn't afraid to go deeper into the forest. I know that I love you, that's why I want to help you get what you want." Little brother kept talking, even when little sister almost knocked him down with a hug.

"We need to stop looking at what doesn't matter, and instead just pay attention to what is important, what matters."

And with that, the fourth pearl fell into little brother's hand, and his cut did not hurt anymore.

Little sister jumped up and down. "It's like magic!" she exclaimed. "We found all four pearls!"

"We can celebrate when we get back to Merlinda's. We'd better get going, she will be wondering where we are." Big brother was being practical, and his siblings agreed. They were all eager to show their treasures to Merlinda. They felt as if they had won the grand prize in this game!

THE Fourth Pearl

Look at
WHAT
MATTERS,
Not at
WHAT DOESN'T
MATTER.

FourPearlsBook.com

Bringing Home The Pearls

The four squirrels pretty much ran all the way back to Merlinda's. When they got to her home, she was there waiting for them at the front door. "Come in, come in! I've been expecting you," she greeted them with a kind and knowing smile.

The squirrels were so excited, and proud of themselves for delivering to Merlinda all four of the pearls she had hidden.

"Ah, I see you were able to find them all. Very good, sweet squirrels. Now tell me about them."

Big brother started, as usual. He handed his pearl over to Merlinda and when she took it, the pearl promptly disappeared.

"What? What happened? Where did it go?" Big brother was confused and upset.

Merlinda's calm demeanor soothed the squirrel. "The pearl did not go anywhere, dear. You see, these are pearls of wisdom. Wisdom is not attached to any object. Wisdom lives in your mind and heart. Once you have it, it is yours to keep always. You can't lose it."

*Wisdom is not attached to
any object. Wisdom lives
in your mind and heart.*

Big brother let out a deep sigh. "You mean, we weren't really hunting for treasure?"

Merlinda held back a giggle. "My child, yes, you were indeed hunting for treasure. And you found it. Wisdom is far more precious than any jewel. The wisdom you gain in this lifetime is part of your purpose here on earth. You are meant to learn and grow and that's exactly what you did today. By leaps and bounds! Tell me, big brother, what lesson did you learn just before the pearl fell into your possession?" Big brother paused, and thought about it.

"I remember exactly. We were talking about butterflies and birds. How we'd like to fly and sing. But then we realized we really like being squirrels. We realized how much we have and how we are really grateful to be squirrels. I said: We need to look at what we have, not at what we don't have. That's when I got the pearl!"

"Yes, indeed." Merlinda nodded with approval. "Many times we are distracted by the external, by things that we think we want, or that we think will make us happy. But what we need to remember is that we already have everything we really need. When we feel gratitude for all that we have, and all that we are, we know that we are never lacking in anything at all. This is a gift more valuable than gold, or pearls, or anything money can buy."

"Now, I understand little sister is responsible for the next pearl. May I see it, dear one?"

Merlinda held out her hand, and little sister squirrel plopped the pearl into Merlinda's palm, where it disappeared.

"Oh! I was hoping I could keep it! It's so beautiful!" little sister lamented.

"Ah, but you can keep it. It is yours for-ever, for that pearl of wisdom represents your newfound knowledge. What did you learn on your journey?" Merlinda bent down low so that she could look at little sister very closely, eye to eye.

"I learned… well, I learned that we can't get distracted by all the things that others are doing all around us. We have our own job to do, and our own reasons for being anywhere. So, I said: 'We need to look at what we are doing, not what anyone else is doing' and that's when I got the pearl." Little sister's eyes were wide and full of wonder.

Merlinda was pleased. "Yes. That is it. Every creature on this planet has a purpose, and a path to walk in their lifetime. You can only walk your own path. Stay the course and you will reach your goal. We can be distracted by trying to follow someone else's way, thinking they have it easier, or that they know better. But each one of us has to follow our own heart, and make our own choices. Each one of us has to carry on with our own purpose, and learn our own lessons all along the way."

Every creature on this planet has a purpose, and a path to walk in their lifetime.

Little sister was so happy she jumped up on Merlinda's lap and gave her a big squeeze! "Thank you, Merlinda!"

"There's no need to thank me, little beauty. You discovered this pearl all on your own, by staying on your own path!" Melinda gave little sister a gentle squeeze right back.

"And the third pearl? Big sister, I believe you have that one." Merlinda beckoned big sister squirrel over.

"Yes, Merlinda. I found the third pearl, and here it is." Big sister placed the perfect pearl into Merlinda's open hand, and the pearl disappeared.

"It's okay that the pearl is gone, because I have the wisdom that came with it."

"So you do!" Merlinda said, beaming with joy.

"Please share with us the wisdom of the third pearl."

"They were all a little scared – I mean, I was, too. We didn't know if we should go farther into the forest. We never went there before. And there was a stream with water, and all kinds of unknown things. But I figured we needed to be brave. I knew we could somehow take the risk and we'd be fine - and maybe we'd even be great with it because we'd learn something. So, I said that. I said 'We need to look at the opportunities, not at the obstacles.' And then the pearl landed in my hand! Just like that!" Little sister was very animated telling the story.

"It looks like you are all great just like you thought you'd be! Good for you, big sister!" Merlinda explained further.

Fear and uncertainty are undoubtedly distractions for us.

"Fear and uncertainty are undoubtedly distractions for us. They can create obstacles where there are none. However, we can turn any perceived obstacle into an opportunity. We just have to change the way we look at things. Taking opportunities, taking on a challenge, overcoming a fear, stretching where we have set limits on ourselves - these are all things that help us to learn and grow. We are all powerful beings. We are capable of so much. We just have to keep moving forward. This is how we make progress. Sometimes we need to move around, sometimes we need to move through – but in any case, we can take action, and think, use our imagination and creativity. Life presents us with opportunities all the time, but we don't always recognize them, or take them."

Little sister clapped her hands with glee. "I'm going to look for opportunities and I'm going to take them!" Merlinda joined in and clapped her hands as well.

"Now there's just one more pearl. Little brother? Do you have it?" Merlinda smiled at the smallest squirrel.

"Yes, Merlinda. I have the fourth pearl. And I think it was the hardest one to get, but I got it!" he said proudly, using both of his hands to place it into Merlinda's palm, where it disappeared. Little brothers' mouth fell open in amazement.

"You are right, little one. This is the most difficult pearl to find. But you did it, and the wisdom is all yours. Please tell us all of the knowledge that comes with this pearl." Merlinda waved her hand as if to present little brother to his audience.

"We were kind of arguing - about the diamond, or the fake diamond, or whatever that thing was, glass I think. I mean, we couldn't tell if it was real or not. It was kind of like we were arguing about whether it was important or not. And I guess also whether it was valuable or not. And I was thinking that it doesn't matter if it is a diamond or glass, it's just a 'thing' and it's not going to last forever. So, to me things aren't important. They come and go. I lose stuff all the time and it's okay. But what is valuable to me is love. That's what's in my heart. I love my brother and my sisters so much. To me that is what is real."

"That is very wise, young squirrel," Merlinda said quietly.

"I hurt my hand, and they were helping me and I felt the love. And I said: 'We need to look at what matters, and not at what doesn't matter' and then I got the pearl."

"That is absolutely the truth." Merlinda said knowingly. "Not only are we distracted by the things of this world, we can be hypnotized by them as well."

"Yes, I know!" little sister piped up. "They look pretty so then I want them! But then I just want something else later. It keeps going on!"

"Exactly." Merlinda was so proud of her young students for all they had learned. "It is as if there is this veil of illusion placed over our eyes. We see things that we think are real, and we want them. But then we are not satisfied and we want more, or something else, or something bigger, or better. It is a trap that we fall into. We can't help it sometimes, because it is our nature to want to make progress in this life."

"But progress doesn't mean getting a bunch of stuff!" little brother said enthusiastically.

"You are right again, smart squirrel!" Merlinda was delighted with his response. "We need to think about what we really want in life. And when it comes down to it, all of that "stuff" doesn't mean anything. It doesn't matter. It can't make us happy, it can't possibly bring us the things we really want in life. We are best off when we strive for what really matters to us, and each individual must decide that for him or herself. I can tell you this: what matters to us changes as we grow. The more we learn and grow the more we understand what is true and good: love, peace, and wisdom. These things benefit everyone in so many ways. They remind us that we are never alone, that we are all connected to one another, and that everything is just fine, just the way it is. We may want to make changes, and that's a good thing. But what we really want to work towards is more love, more peace, and more wisdom in every situation."

What we really want to work towards is more love, more peace, and more wisdom in every situation.

The four little squirrels beamed with joy. "Do you remember the question I asked you earlier today before you left on your adventure?" Merlinda queried.

The squirrels nodded vigorously. "Yes! You said 'do you want to be happy?' just like that!" they all chattered at the same time.

Merlinda said, "That is correct. And do you have an answer for me now?"

"Oh, yes! The answer is yes! We know for sure we want to be happy now!"

"No," big brother interrupted. "I don't want to be happy."

His siblings were astounded. "What? Why? I don't understand?"

"I don't want to be happy, because I already am happy!" big brother said with a huge grin and a belly laugh.

The squirrels tackled their brother with hugs and laughter.

"It feels good to not want anything. It feels good to be happy!" he said in between laughs.

"Yes, we are happy, too!" the others agreed. They collected themselves and embraced Merlinda.

"I can't wait to share the four pearls with my friends," big sister said, "is that okay?"

"Please! Yes, my dear! The wisdom of the four pearls is meant to be shared. It is meant to be used and enjoyed and it belongs to everyone. Please share as freely as you like!"

Merlinda got some last hugs in before the squirrels scurried out the front door to share their newfound knowledge with the world.

Merlinda stood by the door as she watched the squirrels frolic in the forest. She smiled and mused:

"Today is a beautiful day. A wonderful day! And we've got another one on its way with tomorrow." And with that Merlinda opened her hand to reveal four perfect pearls. She raised her arms and tossed the pearls high above the forest, where they glittered and glistened like the twinkle in her eyes before melting into the sky.

Afterword

Merlinda continues to teach in the forest, and is looking into developing an online course for TransformativeU.com so that she can reach many more beings throughout the land. HGTV is featuring her forest home on one of their holiday specials.

The four squirrels are still happy, although they still need to remind one another of the pearls so that they each stay on course and not get distracted. Big brother and big sister are planning to pursue higher knowledge and have ordered several books from Amazon. Little sister has started a popular "inner beauty" blog and has quite a following on social media. Little brother has gotten into crafting, and is helping Merlinda create a new line of inspirational jewelry.

The First Pearl
What you have.

The First Distraction
What you don't have.

"All the powers in the universe are already ours. It is we who have put our hands before our eyes and cry that it is dark."
-Swami Vivekananda

The First Happiness Principle
Gratitude

The Second Pearl
What you are doing.

The Second Distraction
What anyone else is doing.

*"In the long run, we shape our lives,
and we shape ourselves. The process
never ends until we die. And the
choices we make are ultimately our
own responsibility."*

-Eleanor Roosevelt

The Second Happiness Principle
Focus

The Third Pearl
The opportunities

The Third Distraction
The obstacles.

*"You may not control all the events
that happen to you, but you can
decide not to be reduced by them."*
-Maya Angelou

The Third Happiness Principle
Fortitude

The Fourth Pearl
What matters.

The Fourth Distraction
What doesn't matter.

"You wander from room to room
Hunting for the diamond necklace
That is already around your neck!"
-Jalal-Uddin Rumi

The Fourth Happiness Principle
Faith

About The Author

Lissa Coffey is a lifestyle and wellness expert and the founder of CoffeyTalk. com. Lissa is world renowned for her "Ancient Wisdom, Modern Style" philosophy. She has appeared on The Today Show, Good Morning America, HGTV, and many other national and local media outlets.

A best-selling author, Lissa has written several books, including the bestseller "What's Your Dosha, Baby? Discover the Vedic Way for Compatibility in Life and Love." Deepak Chopra says:

"Coffey brings the timeless wisdom of Ayurveda to a contemporary audience and shows us how to discover more about ourselves and our relationships."

Lissa is also the author of the acclaimed e-course The Ayurveda Experience and she has several e-courses on TransformativeU.com

Lissa was honored with the Dharma Award from AAPNA for "Excellence in Promoting Awareness of Ayurveda." She was awarded a commendation for the Mayor of Los Angeles for her "Outstanding Contribution to the Yoga Community."

Follow Lissa on Social Media

Facebook.com/LissaCoffeyTalk

Twitter.com/coffeytalk

Instagram.com/LissaCoffey

More from the four squirrels:

www.FourPearlsBook.com

Other Titles By
LISSA COFFEY

- The Wisdom Collection: Quotes and Commentary to Cultivate Self-Knowledge

- Weight Loss and Wellness the SV Ayurveda Way: Step-Up Your Sugar and Fat Metabolism (co-authored with Vaidya R.K. Mishra)

- Bhakti: 108 Prayers of Devotion

- Ananda: Discover the Vedic Way to Happiness & Bliss

- The Perfect Balance Diet: 4 Weeks to a Lighter Body, Mind, Spirit & Space

- What's Your Dharma? Discover the Vedic Way to Your Life's Purpose

- CLOSURE and the Law of Relationships: Endings as New Beginnings

- What's Your Dosha, Baby? Discover the Vedic Way for Compatibility in Life and Love

- Freddy Bear's Wakeful Winter

- Feng Shui for Every Day (e-book)

- Getting There: Simple Exercises for Experiencing Joy

- Awakened Parenting: Family Life as a Spiritual Path

- Getting There For Teens: A Guide to Success and Fulfillment Today and Everyday (e-book)

- The Healthy Family Handbook: Natural Remedies for Parents and Children (co-authored with Louise Taylor)

Acknowledgments

Thank you to all the mentors I have had in my life so far: Louise Taylor, Vaidya Mishra, Deepak Chopra, Swami Sarvadevananda, Sue Rubin, and Diana DeFrenza. I feel so blessed and fortunate to have gained wisdom and insight from these wonderful people.

Ray Mawst is a ray of sunshine! This talented artist created the beautiful cover and interior design for this book, and many of my others. I adore you, Ray! Learn more about Ray, and the courses he teaches, and follow him on social media – all the info on his site: RayMawst.com

Thank you to Eric Woolf, our extraordinary webmaster. Thank you to Ophelia, Nancy, Lindsay, Corienne, Linda, and Emma – my awesome team - for everything you do to keep the creativity flowing!

And a special thank you to my husband, Greg. I love being on this life journey with you!

Be a Mentor

I've been a Big Sister through our local chapter of Big Brothers Big Sisters of America three times now. It's an amazing experience! There are so many kids, right in your community, who need mentors.

If you're interested in becoming a mentor, please visit the Big Brothers Big Sisters website for more information, and to find a chapter near you: www.bbbs.org

Help Wildlife

It is important to look after our little squirrel friends and all their buddies in the wild. A wonderful organization that my family and I have worked with is the California Wildlife Center. If you'd like more information about how you can help, please visit their website: www.cawildlife.org

Thank you!
Love,
Lissa

Made in the USA
San Bernardino, CA
10 October 2017